I am a Dolphin

Thanks to Meadow for her good ideas — B.T.

First published in 2009 by New Holland Publishers (NZ) Ltd
Auckland • Sydney • London • Cape Town

www.newhollandpublishers.co.nz

218 Lake Road, Northcote, Auckland 0627, New Zealand
Unit 1, 66 Gibbes Street, Chatswood, NSW 2067, Australia
86–88 Edgware Road, London W2 2EA, United Kingdom
80 McKenzie Street, Cape Town 8001, South Africa

Copyright © 2009 in text: Barbara Todd
Copyright © 2009 in photography: Barbara Todd with the exception
of page 20 Dr Steve Dawson; author photo Roger Sutherland
Copyright © 2009 in illustration: Helen Taylor
Copyright © 2009 New Holland Publishers (NZ) Ltd
Barbara Todd has asserted her right to be identified as the author
of this work.

Publishing manager: Christine Thomson
Commissioned by Louise Armstrong
Editor: Georgina McWhirter
Design: Vasanti Unka

National Library of New Zealand Cataloguing-in-Publication Data

Todd, Barbara, 1941-
I am a dolphin / written by Barbara Todd ; illustrated by Helen Taylor.
(I am a--)
ISBN 978-1-86966-264-6
1. Dolphins—Juvenile literature. [1. Dolphins.] I. Taylor, Helen J.
(Helen Joy), 1968- II. Title. III. Series.
599.53—dc 22

10 9 8 7 6 5 4 3 2

Colour reproduction by Pica Digital Pte Ltd, Singapore
Printed in China by Toppan Leefung, on paper sourced from
sustainable forests.

All rights reserved. No part of this publication may be reproduced,
stored in a retrieval system, or transmitted in any form or by any
means, electronic, mechanical, photocopying, recording or otherwise,
without the prior permission of the publishers and copyright holders.

Also in this series:

I am a Penguin
ISBN 978 1 86966 246 2

I am a Seal
ISBN 978 1 86966 287 5

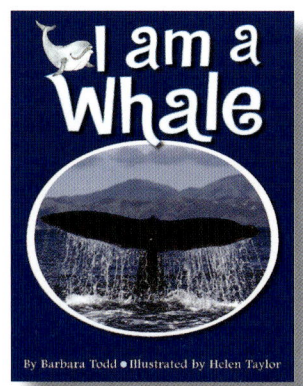
I am a Whale
ISBN 978 1 86966 298 1

I am a Dolphin

By Barbara Todd • Illustrated by Helen Taylor

NEW HOLLAND

I am a dolphin
That lives in the sea
My home has no fences
I'm wild and I'm free

The fish are my neighbours
The turtles and seals

Great mighty whales
Stingrays and eels

I have flippers for arms
And tail flukes for feet
I breathe through a blowhole
Isn't that neat!

My tail flukes move up
And then they move down
My flippers help steer me
As I swim around

I dive deep in the sea
but as much as I wish
I can't stay down forever
I'm a mammal, NOT a fish

Fish breathe underwater
through small slits called gills
I must come up for air
But that's no big deal

I take a few breaths
Then I'm swimming away
Down into the ocean
To hunt for my prey

I squeak, squeal and click
As I search all around
I must swim really fast
When I chase dinner down

What's on the menu?
All kinds of small fish
Yellow-eyed mullet
Make a nice tasty dish

And squid sure taste good
Though they look kind of funny
But I really don't care
'Cause they fill up my tummy

When I have a baby
It grows right inside me
And then it is born
Tail-first in the sea

I must push my calf up
For its first breath of air
Then I nurse it with milk
For at least half a year

I live in large groups
Brothers, sisters and cousins
Aunties and uncles
And friends by the dozen

We spend time together
All through the day
We feed and we rest
Then we have a good play

But we must be careful
DANGER! BEWARE!
There are things that can harm us
If we don't take care

We must keep a lookout
For propellers on boats
Fish nets and plastic
And rubbish that floats

Not every dolphin
Looks exactly the same
Each type of dolphin
Has its own name

I am a Dusky

I am a Common

I am a Hector's
The tiniest of all of them

I am an Orca

The largest dolphin of all

A male's dorsal fin

Is really, really tall!

Hey, I have no dorsal
Just fancy that!
I'm a right whale dolphin
There's no fin on my back

"Don't worry you're just right!"

I'm an Indo-Pacific Bottlenose
I live close to land
There are places where people
Feed me right from their hand

I'm a Common Bottlenose
I swim further offshore
I'm bigger and rounder
So I eat a bit more

There are all kinds of dolphin
Some large and some small
We live right round the world
Thirty-six types in all

We are all dolphins
That live in the sea
Help keep us safe
So we can stay free

Did you know?

- Dolphins, like people, are mammals. All mammals breathe air and are warm-blooded. They give birth to live babies and feed them with milk.

- Dolphins, whales and porpoises belong to a group of mammals called cetaceans. Scientists currently recognise at least 85 different species (types) of cetacean. This number changes every year or so as researchers who study whales and dolphins learn more about them.

- There are 36 cetacean species that are known as oceanic dolphins. These dolphins live mainly in the sea, although a few also spend time in freshwater rivers and lakes. The largest of the oceanic dolphins is the Orca.

- Five additional dolphin species are known as river dolphins because most of them live in rivers. Most river dolphins have tiny eyes and cannot see very well. Amazon river dolphins are known as the 'pink' dolphins. Many of them are part grey and part pink, but a few are pink all over!

- Dolphins live in groups. Some groups are large and some are small. A group of dolphins is called a school or a pod.

- How do dolphins find their way around underwater, where it's often too dark to see? They send out sound waves from the front of their head, and when the sound waves hit a solid object, like a fish or a rock, they bounce back to the dolphins. This is known as echolocation. Each time the dolphin sends out a sound wave, you hear a 'click'. When a dolphin sends out lots of sound waves close together, it makes a fast 'click, click, click,

click' sound. Dolphins are very clever. They can listen to the way the sound bounces back and can tell what's there. The echo from a fish sounds different from the echo from a rock, a squid or another dolphin. Baby dolphins learn the meaning of different sounds the way human babies learn the meaning of different words.

• Dolphins communicate and find their prey by using echolocation clicks, squeaks and squeals. Sometimes it gets very noisy underwater when they are chasing their dinner down!

• Some dolphins, like Hector's Dolphins, live for only 20 years or so, while other dolphins, like Orca, live to be almost 100!

• Hector's Dolphins are found only in New Zealand waters. There are not many left and they could disappear one day if we do not protect them from fishing nets and other rubbish in the water.

• Orca are also known as Killer Whales. They got this name because they eat almost everything. They usually munch on fish and squid, but some Orca also eat penguins, seals, other dolphins, and even whales. But don't worry – Orca don't eat humans!

• Risso's, Striped, Spotted, Hourglass and Spinners are just some of the other dolphins that are found around the world. Spinners are fun to watch. They love to leap into the air and spin round and round. One Spinner spun around seven times during one leap. Do you think he got dizzy?

Teacher/Parent Notes

Try these activities with your children for added learning and lots of fun!

Talk about mammals and some of their characteristics (see page 30). Compare dolphins with fish. Fish are cold-blooded, lay eggs and breathe underwater. What other differences are there? One difference is that a fish's head, body and tail fins move from side to side as it swims through the water, whereas a dolphin's tail flukes move up and down. Get children to make these movements with their bodies. Which way is easier? It's hard to wiggle your body like a fish!

Talk about and compare dolphin families and human families. Ask children to think of all the people who would live with them if all of their extended family – aunts, uncles, cousins – lived and travelled together, like dolphins. Count how many people would be living in the house and think about the changes to everyday life that would need to be made to accommodate these extra people. Think of the advantages and the disadvantages. Get children to draw their house with this new large 'pod' of humans living inside.

Seeing with sound 1: Dolphins rely partly on sound to navigate. But what do we mean by 'seeing with sound'? Blindfold a child (the 'dolphin') and place him/her in the centre of a circle of 'dolphin friends'. Have one friend call out 'hello'. The 'dolphin' in the middle must point in the direction the sound came from and identify the person from the sound of their voice. Let children take turns at being the blindfolded dolphin.

Seeing with sound 2: Continue the experiment to help kids understand echolocation (how dolphins use sound waves to navigate). The blindfolded dolphin is hungry and looking for dinner. It's dark, so he must use echolocation to find his food. When a dolphin sends out sound waves, they sound like clicks. You can give the blindfolded dolphin a musical clacker or another object that represents his clicks. The children in the circle are objects in the sea. Give each child an object that makes a different sound. A fish might be a bell, a squid might be two wooden blocks, an Orca might be a whistle, and a rock might be a clap of the hands. The dolphin faces in a direction and clicks, sending out sound waves. The person he/she is facing makes a sound back (this is the echo of the dolphin's clicks bouncing back). The dolphin must interpret the sound and decide if it is something good to eat or something to avoid. Begin with a few objects, especially with young children, and add more as they get better at interpreting sounds as objects.

The long and short of it: Write down the length of the smallest dolphin (Hector's) and the largest (Orca). Using a ball of string or wool, have one person stand where the dolphin's beak will be and others where they think the tail will be. Use a tape measure to see who is closest. If you're outdoors, use chalk instead, and draw outlines of the dolphins you have measured.

Blowhole experiment: When dolphins breathe, they look as if they are spraying out water, but what is really coming out of their blowhole is air! When the dolphin's warm breath hits the colder outside temperature it condenses into water droplets. Have children blow on a mirror to see how wet their breath really is. Put a second mirror in the fridge for a few minutes and compare breathing on a cold mirror.